ABSENT AND PRESENT

# Absent and Present

## Chester Kallman

*Wesleyan University Press* MIDDLETOWN, CONNECTICUT

Grateful acknowledgments are made to the editors of *Encounter, Listen, Locus Solus,* and *Semi-Colon,* in whose pages some of these poems first appeared.

LIBRARY OF CONGRESS CATALOG CARD NUMBER: 63-8859
MANUFACTURED IN THE UNITED STATES OF AMERICA
FIRST EDITION

Dedicated to W. H. AUDEN
What more could any poet wish to do
Than dedicate his time, in time like you
To grow and grow unfashionable too?

# Table of Contents

FOOD FOR THOUGHT

## A Toast

Cockaigne, Cockaigne, my dearest Long-ago,
My darling Once-upon-a-time,
The lights are dim
And we are here to eat,
Drink and you-know-what.
There are no flavors to disturb us, so
What if the trees are sapless, what if we,
After the bill is left unpaid
And nothing said,
Sprawl on our backs about
The exhausted pot,
Laid out like points of stars we never see?

*The Child is father of the Man . . .*

No one was there.
The curtains were drawn,
My stomach grown
Heavier bare,
Tobacco flecks lay through
The pubic hair.
Natural man,
Where are you?

Behind a fence
Two nine-year-old
Physicians played
With touching innocence;
The probes we made
Were quickly healed
For probing held
A sovereign aid.

So close to the bone
And yet no dangerous game
For nobody came
To take it to heart:
It lies beyond art
How kids can take on
And take off the part
Of woman or man.

Let muscle, let hair
And improper size
Once disguise
The baby though,
The wish to explore
No longer is touch and go,
The wish to cure
Lovingly dies.

Oh Love, dear god, how we
Went seek, poke,
Tickle and stroke
In your name, for your sake
Domestically
Learned to cook
And with booze and smoke
Talk, talk.

But it's hard to believe
The affectionate lines
That seldom vary
From love to love,
That never can carry
The weight we crave
To reassure the signs
Of minor declines.

Even so, how come
I dare subject
Lovers to proof and expect
Good faith of them
When I hardly dare
Begin to reflect
On who I am
With no one there?

No one was there.
My stomach grown
Heavier, are
You the mature
Ultimate buffer
For baby nerve and bone
That would not suffer
The probing lover?

No one was there.
In a night without a mirror
Did I in terror
Of losing face
Begin to bear
What could displace
A greater nearer
Personal space?

As I lay sleeping
At the break of day
A treble voice asked: *Why*
*Should the cost of keeping*
*A lover be*
*Astronomic?*
*Why is a weeping*
*Fat man comic?*

And gently slipping
Bounds to pass
Into a squat
Incubus,
All I once was
On me begot
This dear little pot
Of unlovely dripping.

Am I who sired
With no great fever
This brat required
To watch it take over
Without offense
And to lug forever
Till dead its tired
Hankering innocence?

Must I serve to replete
This not-so-sweet
Young thing-I-once-was by degrees
With delicacies
It once wouldn't eat
And cannot hope
Nowadays to keep
In decent shape?

You there, tubby
Inheritor
Of dubious youth,
I see well who you are,
You downy boor,
You rather grubby
Naked truth
With an old sweet tooth.

No salad days for you
While you're with me.
Oh no, my pet:
Richly you'd eat
Till eventually
You block my view
Of what despite
Your cautions grew.

But Master Big,
On what were you nursed
That a peasant faith
Sustains your growth?
You're sunk if I hold my breath
My greed or thirst,
Or sweat like a pig
Or cram till you burst.

It's true so far
You haven't gone wild
And eaten me broke,
But what are you for,
Unnatural child?
*Love.* Who spoke?
No one was there.
That was the point of the joke.

Toasty-warm on the lawn to lounge and brood
On ten years' bills of fare: Now, here's the one!
A Maytime couple dallies off to the wood
    From sight and sun.

The spirit is less than willing. What keeps young?
One dish of all so vivid that really now
Its eager sauce curls back the pensive tongue
    And sweats from the brow.

Adoringly, when amid summer the first keen
Feel of autumn cuts, my sight
Tingles to mow the inspiring prospect clean,
Roots and all, heaven-sent,
Attendant out there to stock this nice machine
Of visionary appetite.
How neatly I grasp the Japanese who wait
Their widely grubbed nourishment
Till it repose a lotus on the plate
Then peck at it with design. To cull
Sympathetic magic, that's to create
A live world of one's very own,
Compass it, rule it, find it good, insist
It all be finally edible:
Well then, now I must be, if indeed I exist,
You, Nebuchadnezzar, lone
Miscomprehended pantheist.

Since I am everywhere, my doubt is where
Most fully I picture me:
Shorn laurel bound over thinning hair,
A fungus nibbler; gouging a nook
Out of my hedgerow; some lovable honey bear
Unstung; the honey; that humped bee
Working away at a squashed sweaty haw;
The Lord's cuckoo; His chief cook
Boiling down jelly out of tooth and claw;
Avid in service, hills on my platter
Tilted at the one starry maw;
The rose when its glory is to hide
This cool plump customer

Who seasons it to fall. Oh well, no matter:
We'll powder each stone, melt ore, show in the tide.
Good. Good. When tidier,
A screen becomes a suicide.

CITY AND COUNTRY BEASTS

In human scale, the ant each day
About the globe would make his way
    In search of winter meals;
I've watched him hoist a mastodon
Up to his head while dragging on
    A redwood with his heels;
He seldom sleeps, he never sits
Nor ever reaps the benefits
    Of charity appeals:
And men who emulate with love
The ant are soon the victims of
    Impossible ideals.

*Those who are wise, contrariwise,*
*Working upon the human-size*
    *Artful idealization*
    *Of natural inclination,*
*Find a platonic compromise:*
    *My illustration:*

His strength tenfold with purity,
Before each deed of gallantry
    In errantry, the knight
Would sing his love a serenade
Upon the strictest models made
    (He almost got it right);
Then, vows resworn, obeisance done,
He rode into the setting sun
    With lance and armor bright.
Untouchable, his lady fair
Turned up her eyes, let down her hair
    And waved him out of sight.

While she, her champion safely sped,
Trod gaily to her lawful bed
    To do as goodwives must, he
Went nipping round a forest track
That quickly darkly brought him back
    A little flushed and dusty.
Between the kitchen mop and pail
He hung his gear upon a nail
    Unamourously, lusty:
Only the haste with which he topped
The sullen aging skivvy stopped
    His armor getting rusty.

*One who relies, to gain his prize,*
*On antlike toil, must shut his eyes*
    *Firmly to its duration*
    *In natural socialization*
*Or he may waver otherwise:*
    *My illustration:*

Alone and in our time lived one
Who while eschewing present fun
         His happiness delayed
Till he could save himself the right
(By working daily at some quite
         Uninteresting trade)
To marry and to domicile
And dress in her accustomed style
         A distant village maid
Who bravely by her window sitting
Had in the meantime at her knitting
         Like chivalry decayed.

*Whether one flies or plods, denies*
*All to oneself or nought, one dies.*
         *Other interpretations*
         *Of natural manifestations*
*Find, if they care to moralize,*
         *Their illustrations.*

Take modest aims, protective hue,
And shun the current point of view
To flatter best your skill:
As swallows cutting low upstream
Over blue, blue tails flickering, seem
To travel swifter still.

To take an example
From this grass-tumbler,
The caterpillar,
Is impossible
For those maintaining
The need for clear-cut
Early training
To be absolute.

Glancing at this
Menagerie
Anthology,
Who'd care to guess
From a thumb-size hedgehog
With the shiny black
Nose of a dog,
The frightened back

Of a tortoise-shell cat,
And cowhide shoes,
That the leaves it chews
To fretwork might
Swell and simmer
In its cushy dead-white
Gut to a summer
Of gaudy flight?

The grasshopper approached the ant
To ask for a Creative Grant:

"My singing made your labors light."
The puzzled ant refused outright:

"Was *that* noise you? I never know
What's on my pocket radio."

Though bird rocks and the Hesperides
Shrinking drown in boiling seas
As Nemesis undoes
Mankind's is-and-was
And the gods too
Are odds to
Crumble,
Bumble
Bees'll
Buzz.

## Party Bird

From the ballroom window the park lay in excellent view,
And the room (except for one yielding section of floor
    That the guests in their measured frivolity
Instinctively circled) was tastefully solid though new.
It was the kind of party that had often been given before:
    Which gave it its particular quality.

Across the park in the diamond-blue dusk fresh lights
Bared the ceilings of other lives or their shades;
    And though everyone apprehended
An underfoot stillness that spurred the dance to new heights,
Few looked when (the trap-door flaps opened by two of the
        maids)
    Our coming-out heiress descended

To a leathery den and the couch a carrion bird
Hid with his crooknecked poise and the scholarly back
    Of an old petitioner hatless:
With one slow red dispeptic glance he stirred
And glided into the dusk from his casual snack
    She had beaten him off with an atlas.

"Oh, Daddy's down there; he's been dead for a while, it's true,
But he'd die if he missed my party; and as for his guest,
    He hadn't got much of him, had he?
If you want the park, you just have to expect a zoo . . ."
Then off with her partner who clutched to himself like
        possessed
    The nubile remainder of Daddy.

He has the popular touch.
At home abroad, at ease with such
As are not quite his class, yet must be granted
A humorous wisdom like his own, innate,
That he can appreciate—
He, when a point is made, the joker young,
And comment is clearly wanted,
Is ready. He begins
By closing the sapid wit about his tongue.
He glances left. He grins.
He glances right. He looks beneath
His chair and it is there:
The potted plant of air,
The laugh he carries everywhere.
He takes it in his teeth
And worries it, he lifts it up
High over his head and shakes it till it dies.
He chokes upon the sap
And wipes his eyes.

Beautiful, beautiful, she will not strive
To match her beauty with more willful virtues,
Knowing the gift is matchless. Let it thrive.
Why let the shadow of one wish denied
Fall there to mark how vainly she had striven?
And how they light perfection, how alive
Her eyes are, lovelier, lucid in her pride
To be unworthy of what God had given.

Reports come in of scattered violence
Making absolutely no sense
From unorganized groups not so much faceless
As somehow raceless
And somehow singing (singing has been banned),
Studiedly offhand though out of hand.
One can't say what they physically destroy
Or how annoy;
But I'm aware at once that logic's no test
Applicable to their protest
Against the logic of our quiet clean
World-wide labor-saving machine
Which bids to last efficiently forever
(Our bakelite minister elects himself by lever).
Oh but the blood knows it cannot. I wait
To enroll in their euphoric hate,
Certain that they will soon solicit me
Instinctively,
Permit me, belonging, to attend soon
Their underground monster rallies. At full moon
Tonight the unbannable wind howls raw
And drums my window with a wounded paw.
Naturally I admit them, know them there
By the disturbed air
Charged with open carnal conspiracy:
Drawer, purse and closet scream for individual liberty.
Instruct me in your ritual that elects,
Your glee's text,
I pray. Soon, soon I feel and understand:
The whirlwind deposits in my hand
A cold collection of rare chicken parts

(Necks, wings, gizzards, livers, hearts)
That I must play upon with a fierce love
To squeeze out their hot anthem of
A world a-coming where "All birds are one bird
And that's a fun bird."

## Wanderer

Shun the stranger, turn from the wanderer's eyes
Where treasured shipwreck beautifully lies
For what is ever strange cannot be true,
No matter how human eyes will ever view
Each visitation of the nighted swan
Out of nothing, who endlessly moves on
Holding the folded waters at her breast
Through lively silences in fantastic quest
Of nothing, moves attentive to the sound
That hums valediction to the almost drowned
Or throbs all night from forges underground.

ABSENCES

## Missing the Sea

For NEIL LITTLE

The Scotch fir, evergreen, is not all green
But shades itself to inner wine-dark, wine
Poured on soil; its green splayed edges whiten
Fronting woodland green more young, hung before
Its own bare center. Surely, lingering outward
In half-light, sibillant, the shaken tiers
Stop time unless the foam-white needles flow
On moonlit shoals, in steady wavering ranks
Of long slow breakers waft the pale dead home
From broken voyages. Surely they gather
On the unprinted sand now gazing back
With infinite longing for infinite
Caresses. A whispering tide withdraws
In shaken silk, Isolde's call: that tryst,
Like being alive, is perilous; like dying,
Its charming genius crudely a *Come back!*
Come back: the fir wants of the shifting sky
No further element of uncertainty.

Battle tamed this land; one acre of blood
Bought one whole acre of equanimity
And year by year was parceled out to all,
Whereof the rose is emblem and not sign.
From endless journey I awake in darkness
Slowly to hear companionable rain
Or hear the rising wind that shares with rain
Coniferous music, music in growing things,
Unpeopled, personal; and I may sleep
In this dear peace again. The nightingale
Builds no nest in fir tree or in pine;
Marking familiar properties, the dead,
Within horizons that do not buck and run,
Are planted where they always will remain.

*39*

Bless the bright morning! Surely this garden
Reborn of darkness is blackbird song, the courting
Blackbird a younger garden sings, and deep
In the long-shadowed wood two crystal notes
Of lingering rain swell at a twig's end, drop
To cuckoo at their domestic echo, to our
Time-keeping toy. Hawks frame a picture gulls
Never have crossed nor heard; no, gulls cry deserts,
Playpens of burning stone, rejected bottles
Rubbing at salt-gnawed pierheads ringed with oil;
And breed no echo, only one reply:
The longing heart beats, beats *Not I! Not I!*
Time is partitioned by the cuckoo clock.
I measure time in tides, I school my ear
Upon the conch's animated roar.

Surely there is much in having come here:
Shading itself, the fir points noonward; here
A fallen blossom like a boatless sail
Skims over the pond between walking flies
And one unruffled brown-edged water lily;
Here even so the heart cannot but choose
To drink a darker meaning of the rose.

Drop all wish to sing
The slow quickening
Of Apollonian spring.

Sea here also is blue
Though hardly that sea you
Not long ago knew.
You are seen differently.

All is oversung:
Floes launch roars
In some outlandish tongue;
Winter dies rashly.
Restraint serves the young.

Wines of this volcanic shore
Doze in the soil, so brief is
Their probability.
Like love? Well, it may be
You must learn to love yourself
At the close cunningly.

You will entertain
Certain poor weather;
Fresh courtesies will
Sprout with violence.
Can any love explain
Why gulls, glass-eyed, strain
Towards North Cape dumbly?

Can you, at hard mirrors
For whole months lit,
Keep sense enough not to go blind?
Even returning south
You will tote the reflection
Of more props left behind;
Lemming and lizard already
Scuttle paired when you mind.

My rival pens a willingness to lease
My love to me on sympathetic terms.
Come come, my ducks, what's happened to your piece
    Of earthly paradise?
Should I applaud the apple or its worms?

Of course I'm tickled finding I succeed
In touching my successor—is it skill?—
But I don't really grasp the vital need
    For trading our dear dead
With one I've known as good and long wished ill.

## An Encounter

Yesterday evening at the bar I was, I
Must say, at my best entertaining friends with
Stories of absent friends; and it was during
What I can only describe as a bit that was
    Really inventive

That an elderly lady with the bluest
Kindliest eyes and the most bright white hair, turned
Round from her seat to compliment my wit: how
Strange to have caught the off-duty attention of
    One of the Furies.

# Haircut

Recalling that my hair will continue to grow
After I shall have died, it seems
To me only just for a crowning glory,
If not for long. The click and whirr
At my ears sound a man's labor for time
Lightening piecemeal the memento mori
Which still can enthrall images and dreams.
Months drop to each white-smocked shoulder.
Shall I not rise refitted for the chase
    A mere blank older?

By the sunless pool of an all too
Marble Diana in Caserta's gardens
A pre-ruined Pompeiian arcade
Has been built underground with a view
Through its crafty dilapidations
Of umbrella pines sheer overhead:
Such works, tastefully conceived
Out of native excavations,
Waken bland foreshadowings
    Of the best in being dead.

# Berlioz at Saint-Eynard

*Above Meylan lies a little white villa with a far-reaching outlook over the valley. . . . This villa belonged to Madame Gautier, who used to spend the summer there with two nieces, the younger of whom was called Estelle. . . . I fell in love with her . . . no after-loves can blot out the first. . . . I caught sight of Saint-Eynard in the distance, the little white villa . . . I still loved her . . . I heard that she was married . . . and all the rest of it. . . . Old Saint-Eynard, heaven of my star, farewell! . . . The current of Time bears me onward. Farewell, Stella . . . Stella!*

BERLIOZ: *Autobiography*

Should he not, who else was alive to air
In pure expression even one such day?
Behind the squirrel's coarse chatter, hectoring jay,
Who'd note the covened witches' bicker where
With hop or plunge they spanned a sharper blue?
Who'd sing it in her praise? Sheer on the edge
Of yon high cliff her white house gleamed, his true
Wild goddess's: in place, assuredly
A shrine; her very name, Stella, his pledge
Of glorious unavailability.
Autumn drew altar flames from every altering tree.

Her being held every reason to rejoice.
No constant gift of his would learn despair
Though she adored embellishing an air
With beaded nothings in a bitsy voice
Or lapsed away to tear into a dance
Or swooning in cabriolets would settle back
Willingly victimized by circumstance
Flat on its cold cracked leather, loosely tame,
To match the humdrum cadence of the hack:
That was for others; he would keep the flame
Before the virginal demands of her true name.

*46*

Yet, calculating all, he'd not forecast
His heart's chilled logic. How, even so, how
Could she have? Grief tore him like a plough
And would when each new critical winter passed
Into renewals of that harrowing
Huge unkillable need ripely to expose
The still unplumbed nobilities, to sing:
Far better then to sob in her inspired air
Than dryly to be banished into prose.
Her rumored Paris waited, his to dare
Armed with a name, an old guitar and flaming hair.

## The Only Child: Theme and Variations

To H. K.

At the birthday party nobody came to
Twenty blobs of raspberry jello stood
In two rows settling into small red pools.

1.

It is the pine reflected, is the shade
Blotting the mirror clean,
No plumbings made
Which scrape the mean
Unstable slime weighed with discarded tools,
Measure the depth of woodland pools.

The day was clear. Myself I did not love
And found no wish to drink
Or pend above
That various brink
Compelled to wonder where the axe can fall
Leaving no injury at all;

Yet bore delay to hold my kinderkin
In shallow water drowned.
Beloved twin,
The depth you sound
Still still where the axe uselessly fell
Leaving no injury, is hell.

2.

*I'm here, I love.* The thought beguiles
Awakening till awakening asks
What uncompleted tasks,

Joys, rejection slips, come-on smiles,
What murderous breakfast squabbles, queer
Coincidences, choices, blues,
What fruits of labor, and whose,
Brought you to love and settle here;

Asks why this other only one
By whom love has your days
And nights possessed, as though to avoid
Self-consciously reflecting on
Your roused possessive gaze,
Lies parallel to you half-dead.

3.
"Somebody's collecting garbage twenty times a day."
"Once things get going they'll take everything away."

4.
It takes ten days to kill a mother
On a double bed.
Once only, he remembers,
Her one son visited.

Blood, that feeds and drains the soul
And shakes the wedding band,
Served her heart with a dead object
It could not keep in hand.

The dance of life in close quarters
May well turn on a dime;
I might, who knows, have saved her
Could I return in time.

5.

A speculation then. It didn't happen.
It didn't happen. The hissing ebb. My friends.
One day of storms. Boats three times a day.
Time snacks on leftovers. A form of healing.

6.

Beyond their cross-chat, dining late,
King of the table, I watched the door
Of their bar for whatsoever more.
You entered, their friend. Good God! enough
Old solitude marked the awed elate
Onset of unreflecting love
For me: had I to speculate
Still still on what the moment bore,
Blotting our miracle before
Its colors rose in claim? Why prove
How wonders breed in parallel?
Love inscribes the door to hell.
Must blood, exemplary wonder, spur
Its host, as life, to circulate?

7.

Was born with red hair I later
Lost and replaced with gold,
Which pleased mother much better,
So I'm told.

At three appraised a canary—
"Blue as a lemon, that bird!"
It died. Forgot in a hurry,
So I've heard.

At nine was tied up down the cellar
And shown what love is in a way.
But it's a horse of a different color.
So they say.

8.
The game is Solitaire. When the cards baffle you,
Cheating is human like one-and-one makes two.

9.
They were and are where
They've always been: at play in their
Particular God's open air.

How quickly their day goes,
Facing a wall or each other in rows,
Bent solely on hits, catches and throws,

A ball relating their knack
For anticipating in attack
Where it probably will fly back!

It almost would seem their day
Of particular friendships in fair play
Had no other appetite to obey,

That the black mickeys kept hot
Under bonfired orange crates were not
Intended for their empty lot.

*Supper! Come home!* The shapes
Of mothers leaning out through drapes
Are blurred with steam. On fire escapes,

Potted sweet basil dies.
The ball bounds yet, the ball flies
More quickly into colder skies.

*Come home!* They were. They are
Scattered meaninglessly afar
If God is not particular.

10.
My city grew
Contracting into its windy heart like a cabbage:
To me, visiting you
Years later in yours, the dank brimstone assault on
The stairs from twenty flats,
All boiling cabbage, seemed suicidal. What leftovers
Have you to feed your cats?

It's not so hard
Keeping a native gusto alive. In my city
I have a small back yard
For dropping garbage into, a cat's realm for survey;
All theirs to rout for food:
Each prowls wrapped in a unique savagery, each litters
Its own Great Birnam Wood.

11.
Places were set for two. You're late.
Night falls. I dare not watch the door
Nor judge your absence now as more
Than some delay I could not tax

You with nor could you calculate,
Being but innocently lax;
In spite of which, I contemplate
That set-up where, as twice before
To fancies of domestic war,
Impersonally as the axe
Reflecting early sun above
An aging monarch's faithless love,
Three naked bulbs glare back from your
Clean glass, uncalled-for dinner plate.

12.
"No dear, that's not Avernus, that's the edgy spout
Through which the percolated coffee must come out."

13.
Wait. Speak louder. I can't hear you.
Has somebody tapped our telephones?
Who'd dare?
Can't you speak? Is somebody with you there?
Don't be scared that you'll hurt me; I
Am here completely by
Myself now, the tom's off, and mother
Down in the cellar
Whipping up love potions from a bag of old bones.
She, in any case, can bear you,
But the news would hardly kill her
One way or another
Since I must blush for her as well, abashed, when I claim to
Love you and rut, and wonder whatever
It could mean to say that I love her.
We must speak. It's only a hole-in-the-wall:

Liberty Hall,
Dew-drop Inn. There were lots of goodies left over
At the birthday party nobody came to.

Wait. Give me a little time, for that drowned
Silence reminds me the kitchen-sink drain,
Darling, is choked again
And I must do something, you know.
Whenever a big truck passes, there's a sound
From each discarded pot, for years
My souvenirs,
Of wee mouse droppings pattering like seeds.
Must they go?
Later maybe. Give me time:
I swear I'll hustle,
Turn my nose away, jab a fingernail into the slime,
Worry aside swoln fag-ends, *cha* leaves, gristle
Until at last a tepid whirlpool bleeds
Into its proper plumbing. You understand. And she
Downstairs will hear it ruckle by,
Passing by to its destination,
To the sea—
Parent, slumber, separation.
Tell me:
Is it simple or simple-minded to die?

Wait. Do come over. I'll play with you
A game I know that many can play or two:
We'll join hands in a ring,
Count up to twelve like prompt little clocks
And turn into trees
Of the forest. How pure

We are, at peace
In our self-bought surcease,
Soiled underwear
And bedclothes and sour
Dishcloths hang
Freshening
Their winning colors from our limbs,
Rats trim our buried toenails, birds dot our hair;
And the birds will sing
Anthems and hymns.
No, perhaps not: we'll be still still as anything
To watch well how the unmanned axe
Like a woodpecker flies
To his rat-a-tat of mating;
Watch out an age
Till blood curtains our eyes
With its remembered rage
And down to earth, our element, spills
In two rows settling into small red pools.

Wait. Just a bit.
After all we're only human, and that's to the good,
So I'll have to admit
I seem to have slipped in some nice piles of
Haha! My mistake; but I must say
That I honestly could
Have sworn that where I met up with it
Twenty blobs of raspberry jello stood.
Now don't you try to take it away!

No one on earth has the right to; I'll play
Pat-a-cake with the precious stuff
I made and love
As long as I can, not as long as I may.

Wait. And I'll tell you a secret then:
I'm really not me
And you are not my family,
No, a great king was my
Father and his touch turned everything golden.
So there!
My duty's done;
Kiss your precious darling good-bye.
But don't you tell anyone.
Swear!
Don't you lie:
Cross your heart and hope to die.

Wait. The phone's begun ringing next door.
What on earth for?
Could it be you?
But what can I do,
My true love, they,
My friends there, have all gone away
For the winter and locked their apartment. Wait.
Why hasn't our tom returned yet? He's late,

That horny old reprobate
Out for kicks
Whom we may have to fix,
Because the roads are blinding, the woods dim,
And how can I be certain I really hear him
When he caterwauls
Or, trapped, bleeds out his life in calls, recalls, recalls;
Or recognize
His particular glassy yellow eyes?
Come help me. I'll give
The poor dear thing a week to live
If only he ate
Before leaving; well, ten days at any rate:
That much, to bring him home again, I still can wait.

14.
Whose voice is in the wind? My voice
Returning through the woods a cry
The trees must bear to know me by:
Too late. Have I another choice?

Whose earlier instincts ran you wild,
Setting their spoor upon your throat?
All treat it as an anecdote
And smile. Am I the only child?

15.
The day I fell in pebbly tar
On my left knee I wept
Yet see no pain
In this freckled scar
I've kept
Where black tiny blobs remain.

57

She dabbed the scrape near clean through
While blubbering I felt proud
To think no other
Kid I knew
Was endowed
With a real live nurse for a mother.

Gone to earth. You, can you weep
No more bravely now? If no,
Your souvenir
Is found too cheap
To bestow
Much regard upon this late, my dear.

Oh the pity of that regard,
Its comfort as well unless
This knee go bent
So heavily hard
It will press
Down back into her element

As though that soil were years which fell
Between bone and kindred bone,
To touch your fear
That she might well
Disown
This body she gave love, if here

To ask its injured claim, "What indeed
Had mother's orphaned elf
Ever to do
With any need
Himself
For meeting dates or remaining true?

"Has he not played at serving love
With games to suit a host,
Hoping to steal
Authentic stuff
For a ghost
From their tributes to grow real,

"Making them his ghosts? That we can kill
Ourselves alone may be
Profoundly true:
We have and will;
But we
Manage to kill others too."

Now, dear, if you can, remaining where
You are, translate your fey
Position into
An uneasy prayer
To pay
Difference a tribute overdue,

That flesh prevent me, saying *you*,
Meaning some figment of
My selfish fear,
That it be true,
My love,
This late calling you "My dear"

Even as I anticipate
Immediate years lean
And costly, when all
Absent or late
Mean
Will be requiring memorial.

16.
This unloved task remains: never to repeat
A memorable charmed circle. No neat
Endings will help, I must feel each story complete.

I must give its true familiar name to
Estranged love, must keep its particular good
Unglossed. Absence? I must bear witness there were no fools
Present at the birthday party nobody came to.
Twenty blobs of raspberry jello stood
In two rows settling into small red pools?

Well, no matter their meaning now, they were and ceased
In their own time. And then? Let me prepare, at least,
If not a happy, no wasteful or solitary feast.

## Suddenly

Suddenly, quite suddenly, I was without fear:
The buildings were neither too sharp nor too clear:
The staircase sank quietly into its place:
And the watch on my wrist had lost its human face.

**LEFTOVERS**
*Et tout le reste est littérature . . .*

There is an English love that puns itself
In declaration with legalities.
There is a Gallic love that only great
Tacticians have the decency to tell.
There is a German love that loves to die
Proving joined words superior to joined bellies.
There is a polyglot unhappiness
That speaks no living language really well.

Because of an unfortunate event
I bore a Truth, a little accident.
He grew; and now, except that he denies
His shameless parentage, he never lies.

Tales of the folk? Long may their creeds inspire
Uncommon terror, that all may own
What, wrought by one man sitting alone,
May please his neighbors round a common fire.

They feared physicians and sleeping alone the most,
And death was a hovering bother related to both:
The fly that spoilt the summer, the maiden aunt
Whose presence would halt the Athenian conversation.

"Beware" they wrote in margins next to tragic statements;
Were addicted to hands
That, knowing their own, took possession quickly.
They never forgot
The brevity of beauty nor the beauty
Of being brief.

# Notes for an Ars Poetica

Poems take place
In medias res.

\*

Aim for poetic truth, but don't put by
The data of the significant lie.

\*

Poets, like lovers in bed, can lose touch
By thinking too little or thinking too much.†
(Whether scanning the floor, the wall or the ceiling,
For *thinking* above, you can substitute *feeling*.)

\*

The best use for the conversational tone
Is questioning your motives when alone.

\*

It may be the Horatian point of view
Is fitting only for the parvenu.

\*

Odd that so much calculating sense
Is needed for writing with violence.

\*

Originality no doubt
Is something one can't do without
If one lacks a distinctive voice:
The matter is not one of choice.

---

†With acknowledgements to
    "... who thought too little, too much,
  Who were the world's best talkers, in tone and rhythm
  Superb, yet as writers lacked a sense of touch ..."
               MacNeice: *Elegy for Minor Poets*

\*

*To forge a style.* Does that mean *Fraudulently ape*
Or *Work out a garment you never can escape?*
It well could mean instead
*A way to get ahead.*

\*

*Keeping sincerely within one's limitations*
Is the most flattering view of self-imitations.

\*

Style is the genre of one's attitude:
So if you'd sell the world Romantic Poppy,
Conserves from Rome or Cool Beatitude
Or . . . X, you'll hand in advertising copy.

\*

Select a manner you can cultivate;
You'll soon be noted, soon go out of date:
And both events won't say a thing on earth
Of what your writing's ultimately worth.

\*

Our fashions cannot even give advice
On what we must avoid at any price.

\*

To oppose the times it is enough merely
To think personally and compose clearly.

\*

Reflect your times. You will. But make
Yourself more consciously opaque.

\*

You must switch off the news
To hear your bad reviews
Broadcast by the Muse.

\*

You will have work to do. The Muse when heard
Speaks not in grammar but suggestive word.

\*

Spontaneous poems? One might be delighted
Were each line simultaneously recited.

\*

The true beginning is the lonely day
When any poem or poet you adore
Must serve you purely as an ancestor
And not a guide to what you have to say.

\*

As prophets or as poets we
(Call us the nineteen-twenties-born)
Can claim a certain modesty,
But with some pride can also claim
(Call it distinction lightly worn)
Our generation had no name.

\*

Why is it that poets in the critical tongue
Are called *younger* these days to mean older than *young?*

\*

One vision of the literary hell:
A schoolroom packed with poets writing well.

\*

What poems are true?
I know. Don't you?

Rereading *Me*, I notice an abuse
Of certain words in thoughtful over-use
And now propose, for better or for worse,
Divorcing them from uncommitted verse:

*Dear* must with *light, bear* exile for their ease
As wry and borrowed ambiguities;
For their attempt to give my thoughts a norm
They do not feel, *define* parts with *inform;*
*That* goes for *this: that* it no longer be
With *one some* ruse to shun portentous *the;*
And *eyes* and *hands,* nerved agents for old *hearts,*
May now relax; I'll grope for other parts
Of speech though doubtful I can prove—
Nor could I wish to be so—*bright* enough
To forage out new proper rhymes for *love*
Or any mode of writing without Love.